# TRAVEL WITH THE GREAT EXPLORERS

Explore with

# Stanley and Livingstone

Cynthia O'Brien

Crabtree Publishing Company
www.crabtreebooks.com

# Crabtree Publishing Company
## www.crabtreebooks.com

**Author:** Cynthia O'Brien

**Managing Editor:** Tim Cooke

**Designer:** Lynne Lennon

**Picture Manager:** Sophie Mortimer

**Design Manager:** Keith Davis

**Editorial Director:** Lindsey Lowe

**Children's Publisher:** Anne O'Daly

**Crabtree Editorial Director:** Kathy Middleton

**Crabtree Editor:** Petrice Custance

**Proofreader:** Wendy Scavuzzo

**Production coordinator
and prepress technician:** Tammy McGarr

**Print coordinator:** Katherine Berti

Written and produced for Crabtree Publishing Company
by Brown Bear Books

**Photographs:**

**Front Cover: Dreamstime:** cr; **Getty Images:** Hulton Archive
Fototeca Storica Nazionale l; **Shutterstock:** Eric Isselée.

**Interior: Alamy:** AfriPics.com 25b, CH Collection 18b, Classic Image
12-13b, Interfoto 29b, Mary Evans Picture Library 21t, Pictorial Press
Ltd 10tl, 24b, Print Collector 12, Prisma Archivo 11, World History
Archive 15cl; **Angus Library and Archive:** 14; **Getty Images:** Hulton
Archive 22t, Print Collector 10br, UIG 17c; **International Atomic
Energy Agency:** 23b; **istockphoto:** 26; **Library of Congress:** 5t,
25t; **London Missionary Society: National Library of Scotland:**
17b; **Princeton Educational:** Public Archives 6r, 19b; **Shutterstock:**
6bl, Natalya Aksenova 16bc, Everett Historical 5bl, 13t, Anan
Kaewkhammul 16bl, imagIN.gr.photraphy 23l, Marzolino 7b, Giulo
Napolitano 7t, Inna Tixchenko 22b; **SOAS:** The London Missionary
Society 16r, 18t, 19l, 20, 28b; **Thinkstock:** istockphoto 24t, Photos.
com 4, 28t, 29t; **Topfoto:** Fine Art Images HIP 15r, ullsteinbild 21bl,
World History Archive 27t; **UIG:** 17t; **Wellcome Images:** 27b.

All other artwork and maps, **Brown Bear Books Ltd**.

Brown Bear Books has made every attempt to contact the
copyright holder. If you have any information please contact
licensing@brownbearbooks.co.uk

**Library and Archives Canada Cataloguing in Publication**

O'Brien, Cynthia (Cynthia J.), author
    Explore with Stanley and Livingstone / Cynthia O'Brien.

(Travel with the great explorers)
Includes index.
Issued in print and electronic formats.
ISBN 978-0-7787-2848-1 (hardback).--
ISBN 978-0-7787-2852-8 (paperback).--
ISBN 978-1-4271-7727-8 (html)

    1. Stanley, Henry M. (Henry Morton), 1841-1904--Juvenile
literature. 2. Livingstone, David, 1813-1873--Juvenile literature.
3. Africa--Discovery and exploration--Juvenile literature. I. Title.
II. Series: Travel with the great explorers

DT3.O27 2016      j916.70423092'2      C2016-903343-0
                                         C2016-903344-9

**Library of Congress Cataloging-in-Publication Data**

Names: O'Brien, Cynthia (Cynthia J.), author.
Title: Explore with Stanley and Livingstone / Cynthia O'Brien.
Description: New York, New York : Crabtree Publishing Company, [2016] |
    Series: Travel with the great explorers | Includes index.
Identifiers: LCCN 2016023866 (print) | LCCN 2016024085 (ebook) |
    ISBN 9780778728481 (reinforced library binding) |
    ISBN 9780778728528 (pbk.) |
    ISBN 9781427177278 (electronic HTML)
Subjects: LCSH: Stanley, Henry M. (Henry Morton), 1841-1904--Juvenile
    literature. | Livingstone, David, 1813-1873--Juvenile literature. |
    Africa--Discovery and exploration--Juvenile literature.
Classification: LCC DT351.S6 O27 2016 (print) | LCC DT351.S6 (ebook) |
    DDC 916.704/230922 [B] --dc23
LC record available at https://lccn.loc.gov/2016023866

## Crabtree Publishing Company
www.crabtreebooks.com    1-800-387-7650

Printed in Canada/072016/EF20160630

**Published in Canada**
**Crabtree Publishing**
616 Welland Ave.
St. Catharines, ON
L2M 5V6

**Published in the United States**
**Crabtree Publishing**
PMB 59051
350 Fifth Avenue, 59th Floor
New York, New York 10118

**Published in the United Kingdom**
**Crabtree Publishing**
Maritime House
Basin Road North, Hove
BN41 1WR

**Published in Australia**
**Crabtree Publishing**
3 Charles Street
Coburg North
VIC, 3058

# CONTENTS

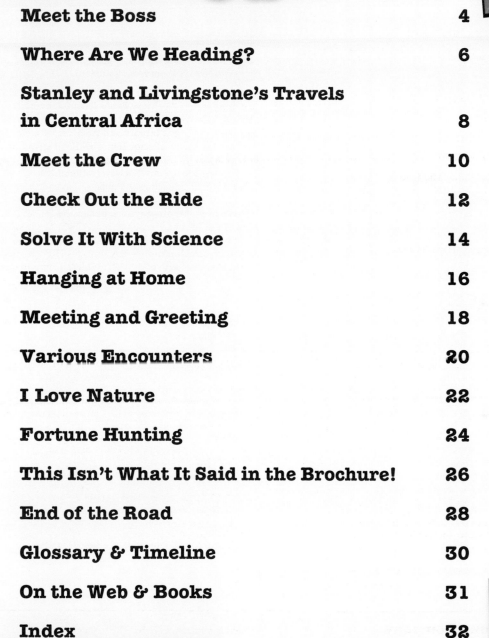

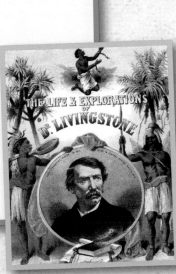

# Meet the Boss

Before their historic meeting in Africa in 1871, the Scottish explorer David Livingstone and Welsh-born American Henry M. Stanley led very different lives.

## MISSION AFRICA

**+ Livingstone aims to spread the word**

David Livingstone was born in Scotland in 1813. He started working at a cotton mill when he was just 10 years old. At age 23, he started training to be a doctor, and later studied at the London **Missionary** Society. After receiving his medical license and becoming an **ordained** missionary in 1840, Livingstone hoped to travel to China. However, Britain and China were at war. The Society sent Livingstone to South Africa, instead.

THE LIFE & EXPLORATIONS OF DR. LIVINGSTONE

## CAN I GET AN AUTOGRAPH?

**★ Britain hails heroic explorer**

Livingstone arrived in South Africa in 1841. For 10 years, he set up **missions** in southern Africa. Apart from his missionary work, Livingstone hoped to end the slave trade by finding other trade opportunities. In 1853, he set off to cross Africa from east to west. When he got back to England in 1856, he was famous. Livingstone returned to Africa in 1858 to continue exploring.

> If you have men who will only come if they know there is a good road, I don't want them. I want men who will come if there is no road at all." *Livingstone describes the adventurous spirit he wanted in the men who joined his expeditions.*

# MISSING!

+ **Livingstone feared dead**

+ **Lost in Africa**

In 1866, Livingstone traveled east from Zanzibar to search for the source of the Nile River. Rumors spread that Livingstone had died, so the Royal Geographical Society sent a search party. They did not find the missing doctor. There was no word from him until a letter, written in May at Ujiji, arrived in Zanzibar in October 1869. Then he disappeared again. It seemed that Livingstone had vanished.

## BULA MATARI

☞ **Rowlands reinvents himself**

☞ **War veteran loves adventure**

John Rowlands was born in Wales in 1841. He lived in a **workhouse** as a child. At age 18, he left Britain for a new life in the United States. He met a merchant at sea and borrowed his name, becoming Henry Morton Stanley. In the United States, Stanley fought on both sides in the Civil War (above), was a sailor, and worked as a journalist in the American West. Later, in Africa, his strong character earned him the name, Bula Matari, which means "Breaker of Rocks."

# FIND LIVINGSTONE!

★ **Newspaper reporter sent to Africa...**

★ **...to prove Livingstone is alive**

Stanley became a reporter for the *New York Herald* newspaper. He wrote about a British war in Abyssinia, now Ethiopia, and other conflicts. The paper sent Stanley (left) to Africa to find David Livingstone. The British explorer had been missing for years. Finding him would be a great **scoop** for the *Herald*. Stanley vowed to find Livingstone or bring back proof that he had died.

# Where Are We Heading?

Livingstone and Stanley's travels revealed the heart of Africa to the rest of the world. They crossed dangerous swamps and deserts, explored vast lakes, and sailed along powerful rivers.

## WHAT'S OUT THERE?

- ☞ Journeys in an unknown land
- ☞ Filling in the blanks

In the mid-1800s, Europeans knew so little about the **interior** of Africa that they called it the "Dark Continent." They left it blank on maps because they did not know what was there (right). Livingstone and Stanley changed all that. They described a diverse land, from the rain forests of the Congo to the mighty Zambezi River and the sandy shores of Lake Tanganyika.

A NEW MAP OF AFRICA FROM THE LATEST AUTHORITIES. By JOHN CARY Engraver 1805.

## MAJESTIC FALLS

+ First European to see spectacular waterfall

In 1858, Livingstone began his journey west across Africa by traveling along the Upper Zambezi River. On his return east along the Lower Zambezi, he arrived at a spectacular waterfall (left). The local people called it Mosi-oa-Tunya, which means " the smoke that thunders." Livingstone renamed it Victoria Falls, in honor of the British queen.

# AFRICA'S GREAT LAKE

## + Exploring Lake Tanganyika

Livingstone spent his last years exploring Africa's largest lake, Tanganyika (right). He thought it might be the source of the Nile River, but then discovered that he was wrong. Livingstone was resting at Ujiji, on the shores of Lake Tanganyika, when Stanley found him.

# IT'S A MYSTERY

★ **Seeking the river's source**

★ **Explorers' claims differ**

The British hoped that the Nile River might provide a trade route north through Africa, so they were eager to find its source. In 1858, the explorer John Hanning Speke declared that the Nile began at a lake he named Victoria. Another explorer, Richard Burton, said the source was Lake Tanganyika. Livingstone set out to solve the mystery in 1866, but could not. Years later, Stanley confirmed Speke's findings. It is now known that the White Nile flows from Lake Victoria at Ripon Falls.

# SLAVE TOWN

## ☛ Refuge with the Arabs

Tabora is now a town in Tanzania. In the 1800s, it was the hub of the slave trade run by Arabs. It was also a center of African resistance to the trade. Stanley and Livingstone both stayed at Tabora in 1871. At separate times, they stayed just outside the town in a *tembe*, or fortified house (below). The two men returned to Tabora together in 1872.

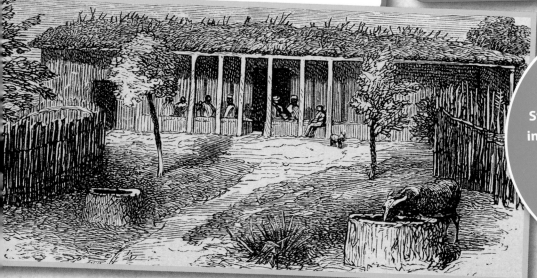

## Did you know?

Stanley's search for Livingstone included a five-day trek through knee-deep black water in the 45-mile (72 km) long Makata Swamp. A porter, the group's donkeys, and a dog all died of dysentery.

# STANLEY AND LIVINGSTONE'S TRAVELS IN CENTRAL AFRICA

David Livingstone's travels took him into east–central Africa, as did Stanley's mission to find him. Stanley later explored extensively in west–central Africa, but those travels are not shown on this map.

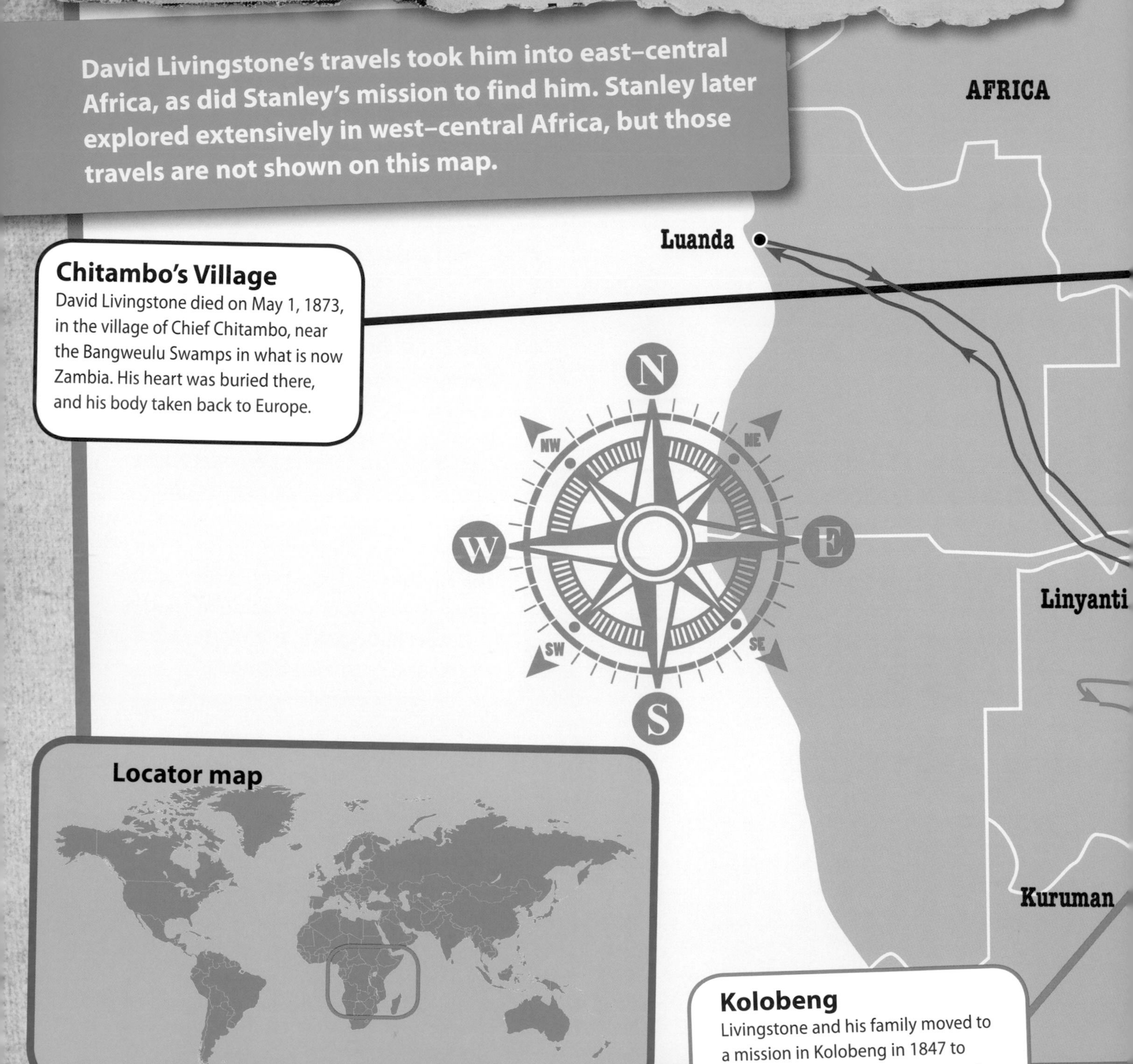

**AFRICA**

Luanda

## Chitambo's Village
David Livingstone died on May 1, 1873, in the village of Chief Chitambo, near the Bangweulu Swamps in what is now Zambia. His heart was buried there, and his body taken back to Europe.

N

NW    NE

W    E

SW    SE

S

Linyanti

### Locator map

Kuruman

## Kolobeng
Livingstone and his family moved to a mission in Kolobeng in 1847 to preach to the local Bakwena people.

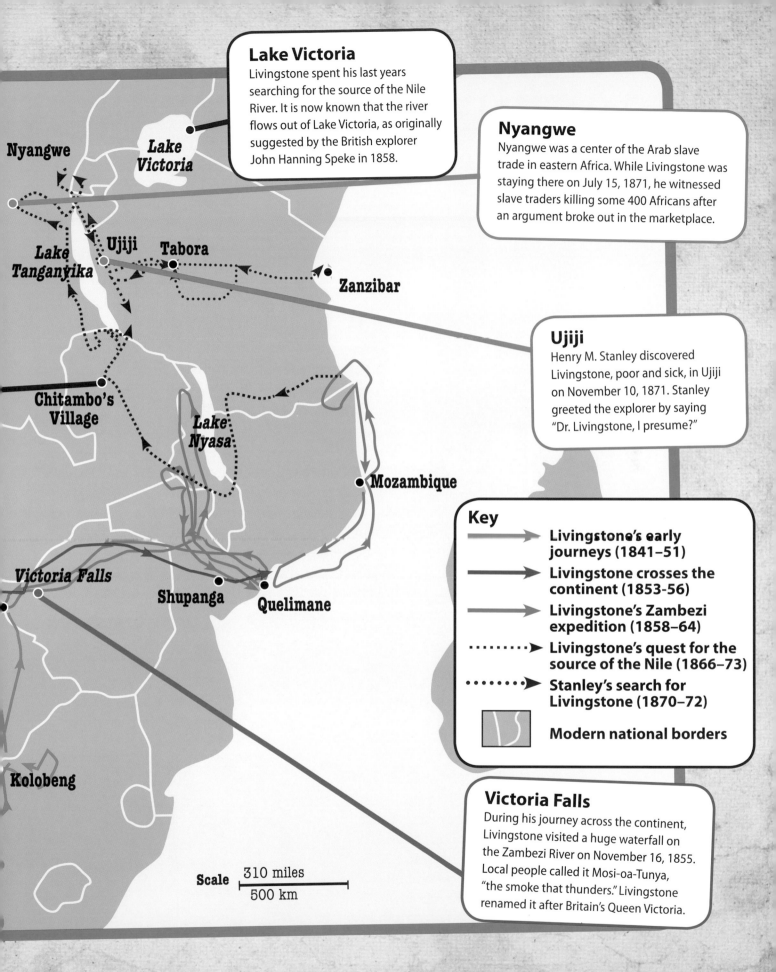

### Lake Victoria
Livingstone spent his last years searching for the source of the Nile River. It is now known that the river flows out of Lake Victoria, as originally suggested by the British explorer John Hanning Speke in 1858.

### Nyangwe
Nyangwe was a center of the Arab slave trade in eastern Africa. While Livingstone was staying there on July 15, 1871, he witnessed slave traders killing some 400 Africans after an argument broke out in the marketplace.

### Ujiji
Henry M. Stanley discovered Livingstone, poor and sick, in Ujiji on November 10, 1871. Stanley greeted the explorer by saying "Dr. Livingstone, I presume?"

### Victoria Falls
During his journey across the continent, Livingstone visited a huge waterfall on the Zambezi River on November 16, 1855. Local people called it Mosi-oa-Tunya, "the smoke that thunders." Livingstone renamed it after Britain's Queen Victoria.

**Map labels:** Nyangwe, Lake Victoria, Lake Tanganyika, Ujiji, Tabora, Zanzibar, Chitambo's Village, Lake Nyasa, Mozambique, Victoria Falls, Shupanga, Quelimane, Kolobeng

### Key
→ **Livingstone's early journeys (1841–51)**
→ **Livingstone crosses the continent (1853-56)**
→ **Livingstone's Zambezi expedition (1858–64)**
······▶ **Livingstone's quest for the source of the Nile (1866–73)**
•••••▶ **Stanley's search for Livingstone (1870–72)**
☐ **Modern national borders**

**Scale** 310 miles / 500 km

# Meet the Crew

## To America

Robert was the Livingstones' eldest child. After his mother died, he could not find his father, who was exploring. Robert sailed to the United States. He fought for the Union in the Civil War. He died in battle in 1864.

Local guides, European scientists, and even soldiers from India were among the people who traveled with Livingstone and Stanley on their expeditions.

## FAMILY AFFAIR

+ Livingstone marries friend's daughter

+ Wife and children endure hardship

In 1845, David Livingstone married Mary Moffat. She was the daughter of another missionary, Robert Moffat. The couple had five children, although one daughter died as a baby. Livingstone sometimes took his family (left) on his travels. Mary traveled widely, even when she was pregnant. She crossed the Kalahari Desert twice. In 1862, after joining David to explore the Zambezi, Mary died of **malaria**.

## LOYAL TO THE END

☛ Young Africans travel with Livingstone

☛ Remain faithful even after death

Two young Africans, James Chuma and Abdullah Susi (right), traveled with Livingstone for many years. Chuma was a cook, while Susi was a **porter**. After Livingstone died, they helped carry his body to Zanzibar. Susi later explored the Congo with Stanley. Both Chuma and Susi went to London to report on Livingstone's final journey. They received medals from the Royal Geographical Society for their services.

# CARRYING THE LOAD

◄ Islanders used for African mission

On his 1866 expedition, Livingstone took 30 porters to help him (below). Twelve of the porters were sepoys—Indian soldiers in the British Army in Bombay. Nine more came from the Comoro Islands, off the east coast of Africa. Livingstone found the islanders unreliable, and most deserted him after a short time.

## My Explorer Journal

★ **Imagine you had the chance to go with David Livingstone on one of his expeditions. How would you be able to help? Perhaps you could cook. Maybe you could help John Kirk by drawing the plants.**

# SIDI MUBARAK BOMBAY

+ Former slave becomes expert guide

Sidi Bombay was a member of the Yao tribe from East Africa. Arab slavers sold him to an Indian master who named him Mubarak. Bombay lived in India for years but when his master died, he returned to Africa as a free man. He worked as a guide for the explorers Richard Burton and John Hanning Speke. He led Stanley's **caravan** on the search for Livingstone. In 1873, Bombay walked from coast to coast across Africa.

# TRAVELING COMPANION

★ Scottish doctor joins Livingstone

★ Kirk studies plant life

John Kirk was a Scottish doctor and **botanist** who joined Livingstone's expedition in 1858. The two men did not always get along, but they traveled together for five years. Kirk's medical and botanical training was useful. He collected many plant specimens to send to Britain. On Livingstone's suggestion, Kirk became vice-consul of Zanzibar in 1866. Later, he was criticized for not sending supplies to Livingstone during his last expedition.

# Check Out the Ride

Livingstone and Stanley preferred to travel in different ways. Livingstone took few companions, while Stanley took hundreds of supporters.

## Did you know?

Livingstone usually traveled on foot. When Stanley met Livingstone in 1871, he gave him a mule. Livingstone was sick, and Stanley designed a special saddle for him.

## TRAVELING LIGHT

+ Bare necessities

+ Carry what you can

Livingstone usually traveled with just a few companions, including young family members, porters, and a cook (right). This small group appeared less threatening to the people he visited. He carried few clothes when traveling. More important were food, medicine, tools, and beads for trading. This and Livingstone's willingness to learn about the languages and customs of different peoples usually made him a welcome guest.

## TRAVEL UPDATE

### Be prepared!

★ If you're heading into East Africa, make sure you have the right gear. One essential is a boat for exploring the region's many rivers. Henry Stanley bought two long, narrow boats in Zanzibar. He replaced the wooden sides with lighter canvas that could be easily folded and carried overland. The keel, ribs, and other pieces were carried by porters. When he came to a river, Stanley could reassemble the boats and continue exploring.

# THE GREAT EXPEDITION

★ **Largest expedition ever**

★ **Almost 200 men on quest**

Stanley organized huge expeditions (right). In 1874, he left Zanzibar to look for Livingstone with 192 men, including 157 local porters (*pagazis*) and 23 soldiers (*askaris*), plus some European companions. The porters carried heavy loads, but there were also 27 donkeys and 2 horses for transportation. It was the largest expedition ever to venture into the interior of Africa.

## BOAT RUNS OUT OF STEAM

☞ **Slow and leaky ship sinks**

☞ **Explorer finds a major river**

In 1858, the British government asked Livingstone to explore the Zambezi River. Livingstone had an iron steamboat built in England to help (left). However, the *Ma Robert*'s engines were too weak for the river's **rapids**, and it eventually sank. Livingstone used a replacement, *The Pioneer*, to explore Lake Nyassa. Mary Livingstone arrived on a third boat, the *Lady Nyassa*. When the government canceled the expedition in 1862, Livingstone sailed the *Lady Nyassa* across the Indian Ocean to Bombay in British India.

## Get Walking!

Experts estimate that Livingstone traveled nearly 30,000 miles (48,280 km) during his exploration of Africa. Most of the time, he traveled on foot!

# Solve It With Science

Livingstone used the latest European medicine to cure people he met on his travels. He also had the most up-to-date navigation equipment.

## TRAVEL UPDATE

### Tools of the trade

If you're heading into new territory, get as much information as possible. Before he headed into Africa's interior where there were no maps to follow, David Livingstone studied navigation with the astronomer Thomas Maclear. He carried modern tools, such as a **chronometer** that kept accurate time, a **compass** to show direction (right), and a thermometer to help judge **altitude**. Livingstone also carried a **sextant**, which helped him navigate by measuring the height of the stars above the horizon.

## TRAVELING DOCTOR

★ Learning from the locals...

★ ... and treating them

Livingstone was a trained doctor. He traveled with a medical chest that contained a **scalpel**, a saw for cutting bones, a tooth extractor, and a **stethoscope**. People traveled long distances to be treated by the European doctor. Livingstone also learned much from local African **medicine men**. They showed him how to use plants to cure illnesses, such as mupanda panda for fever, mutuva for coughs, and munyazi to heal wounds from poisoned arrow tips.

## DON'T LET MALARIA GET YOU DOWN!

- ☞ South American tree...
- ☞ ...enables exploration in Africa

One of the most important medicines Livingstone carried was quinine. It was extracted from the South American cinchona tree's bark (below left). Quinine helped treat malaria, a disease spread by mosquitoes. Livingstone combined quinine, rhubarb, and other ingredients to cure malaria. An English company sold his treatment as tablets named "Livingstone Rousers."

## My Explorer Journal

★Imagine you have to pack a bag to go with Livingstone. He only wants to take the basics. Make a detailed list of the supplies you would want to take with you.

# MAGIC LANTERN

- ★ Biblical light show
- ★ Puts words into pictures

Livingstone was eager to spread the teachings of the Bible, but few Africans at that time could read. Instead, Livingstone showed them illustrations of Bible stories. The pictures were painted onto glass slides that Livingstone inserted into a device called a "magic lantern" (above), which was very popular with the Victorian public. The light inside the box projected a large version of the pictures onto a wall or screen.

# Hanging at Home

Livingstone and Stanley became experts at making themselves as comfortable as possible—even if they were in the middle of a swamp!

## HOME AT KOLOBENG

☛ Founding a mission

☛ Spreading the word

In 1847, Livingstone founded a mission at Kolobeng (right) to preach to the Bakwena people of southern Africa. The Bakwena helped him build homes and a church that doubled as a school. Livingstone showed the Bakwena European methods of farming, such as **irrigation**. He and his family lived in a basic hut for the first year and food was scarce. When a drought forced them to move, Livingstone moved farther into the interior to look for people to **convert**.

## TUCK IN!

+ A warm welcome for Stanley

When Henry Stanley arrived in Tabora in 1871, he stayed at a stone house belonging to an Arab slave trader. There was plenty of room for Stanley and his men. The wealthy Arabs in the area sent Stanley trays full of food, such as curried chicken, pomegranates, lemons, eggs, and rice. They also sent oxen, sheep, goats, and chickens to be killed for meat.

# DON'T CATCH COLD!

Although daytime temperatures in southern Africa can be very hot, especially during the rainy season, at night it can be very cold. On his travels, Henry Stanley usually slept in a hammock inside a tent for warmth. Porters set up the tent and hammock as soon as the expedition arrived at a new campsite.

# DON'T DROP IT!

★ **Stanley carries a bottle**

★ **Celebrates with Livingstone**

Before he left Zanzibar, Stanley bought a bottle of champagne. When he finally found Livingstone at Ujiji, he opened the bottle to celebrate. The two men shared the champagne and ate a very big meal. It was the first good food that Livingstone had eaten in a long time.

# MAN OF LETTERS

☛ **Evenings spent writing**

☛ **Permanent record of trip**

When he was not traveling, David Livingstone spent much of his time writing his journals and letters. He made notes, described what he had seen, and drew maps (below). When he ran out of writing paper, he wrote on anything he could find, such as old sheets of newspaper. When he had used all his ink, he made his own from the juice of berries. Livingstone's writing is not very clear and many of the notes are now so faded they are difficult to read. Recently, scientists have used special cameras and dyes to help them to read the explorer's journals.

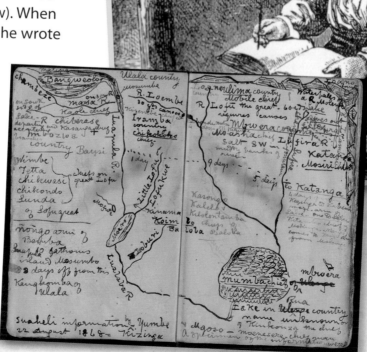

# Meeting and Greeting

When Livingstone arrived in Africa, he started learning the local languages and customs. This helped him to understand and communicate with the people he met.

## THE SOUTHERN PEOPLE

- Spreading the word in the south
- Livingstone learns languages

Livingstone lived among the Bakwena, a Tswana people, for four years and learned their language. The Bakwena moved with him to his missions in Chonuane and Kolobeng. Livingstone also preached to other groups, including the Lunda (right). The Lunda did not welcome foreigners, but Livingstone showed them he was not a threat.

## A CONVERT

★ Chief turns to Christianity

★ Becomes a missionary

The ruler of the Bakwena was Sechele (left). He met Livingstone in 1847. Livingstone taught Sechele to read, and introduced him to European farming methods. After Livingstone persuaded Sechele to divorce four of his five wives, he **baptized** the chief as a Christian in 1848. Sechele was Livingstone's only convert, but the chief went on to convert the Bakwena and other peoples to Christianity.

# GETTING ALONG

**+ Meeting the Makololo**

**+ A lasting friendship**

The Makololo people lived near Linyanti, on the Zambezi River. Livingstone noticed that some of them wore European clothes and discovered they had traded with Portuguese slavers. The explorer became friends with the Makololo chief, Sebituane, but the chief died just two weeks after the two men first met in 1856. The Makololo people did not forget their chief's friend, however, and helped Livingstone's later explorations.

## Did you know?

According to a Makololo story, Chief Sebituane died after he rode Livingstone's horse. The explorer warned him the horse was difficult to handle, but Sebituane insisted. He was thrown off and died from his injuries.

# TRAVEL UPDATE

## A little help from my friends

★ For traveling in unfamiliar territory, make sure you have some local knowledge! When Livingstone and his family visited the Makololo, Sebituane's son Sekeletu was the chief. He proved to be a good **ally**. He gave Livingstone 33 canoes and supplied men to join the trans-African expedition. Later, Makololo guides and porters also joined Livingstone on his Zambezi River expedition, when he discovered the spectacular waterfalls.

# Various Encounters

On his later travels, Livingstone met different African peoples as well as Arab traders. Stanley met many of the same peoples while looking for Livingstone.

## Wagogo
The Wagogo lived between the coast and Lake Tanganyika. They forced travelers to pay them to cross their lands. Stanley paid them in cloth, called doti, on his way to Ujiji.

## TRADERS FROM ZANZIBAR

- ☛ Arab traders take hold in East Africa
- ☛ Moves slaves in large groups

By the mid-1800s, Arab traders had built a large network in East Africa. They controlled towns such as Ujiji, Tabora, and Nyangwe, which were bases for the trade in slaves and **ivory**. The traders traveled inland from Zanzibar in large caravans. They forced captured Africans to march back to the coast to be sold as slaves.

## THE CHAINS

- ★ Face to face with slavery
- ★ Africans help the Arabs

As Stanley searched for Livingstone, he saw a chained group of slaves on their way to the coast (right). The masters of the slaves were also Africans. Stanley learned that Africans often cooperated with the Arabs in the slave trade by capturing slaves from other African peoples. Both Stanley and Livingstone tried to find ways to stop slavery in Africa—but in the end they helped to increase **colonization**.

# HITCHING A RIDE

**+ Livingstone hates slavery...**

**+ ... but relies on slave traders**

Even though he hated slavery, Livingstone was often forced to rely on Arab slave traders for supplies, protection, and transportation. In 1867, he traveled first with Tippu Tip (or Tib), one of the most powerful traders, then with another trader, Muhammad bin Salim. After Livingstone fell sick, another trader, Bogharib, helped him. When Stanley visited with Livingstone, they were also visited by local Arab traders (below).

## Did you know?

The Wagogo were famous for their unique appearance. They pierced their ear lobes, then inserted wood to stretch the skin. They often inserted **gourds** or other objects into the large holes.

# THE AFRICAN BONAPARTE

☛ **African King terrorizes neighbors**

☛ **Stanley witnesses battle for slave trade**

Mirambo, or Mtyela Kasanda, was a Nyamwezi leader who became powerful by conquering his neighbors, and trading ivory and slaves. He fought the Arabs for control of the trade routes in East Africa. In 1871, Mirambo's warriors (left) attacked Tabora, where Stanley was staying. Stanley called Mirambo the "African Bonaparte," after the famous French military leader Napoleon Bonaparte.

# I Love Nature

## Complaints

Livingstone's books were illustrated by artists who had not seen the animals they drew. One made a lion look larger than a hippo. The explorer said of the drawing, "Anyone who knows what a lion is will die laughing at it."

## WHAT LIES BENEATH

+ Mind the water!

Crossing African rivers and lakes could be dangerous. Hidden threats often lay just below the surface. A sharp-toothed crocodile grabbed and killed Stanley's favorite donkey, Simba, as it tried to cross a river. While Livingstone was traveling on the Zambezi River, a hippopotamus overturned his canoe. Livingstone and his guides were lucky to survive. Hippos are huge animals and are sometimes very aggressive.

## ON THE HUNT

★ Game on the menu...

★ ... as well as locusts!

When Livingstone traveled in what is now Zambia, he wrote, "hundreds of buffaloes and zebras grazed on the open spaces." These animals often provided meat for the explorer, but he also ate another local favorite: locusts (above).

## VARIED CLIMATE

**Before David Livingstone explored, Europeans believed the climate made it impossible for white people to live in Africa. Instead, Livingstone found a pleasant subtropical climate. He learned that southern Africa had hot rainy seasons and mild dry seasons.**

## Did you know?

Livingstone loved the African landscape. "The trees which adorn the banks are magnificent," he wrote in his journal. He said Africa was "the very essence of beauty."

# TINY KILLERS

★ **Insects pose deadly threat**

★ **Cause killer diseases**

Some of the most dangerous creatures Livingstone and Stanley faced were tiny insects. The Anopheles mosquito carried malaria, a disease that causes fever and vomiting. Explorers used quinine as a defense against malaria. A bite from an infected tsetse fly (below) caused sleeping sickness (called trypanosomiasis) in humans. Sufferers became confused and sleepy in the day, and unable to sleep at night. There was no cure for the disease. The explorers slept under nets to avoid being bitten.

# WARNING!

☛ **Tricky monkey kidnaps children!**

☛ **Probably a cheeky chimp**

One of the African animals Livingstone described was a monkey he called a "soko." The explorer drew a picture of the animal, so we can tell it was likely a chimpanzee. According to Livingstone, the soko liked to snatch children for fun, though it quickly let go if it was offered a banana instead. The clever monkey was not easy to catch. It was so "cunning … that no one can stalk him in front without being seen."

# Fortune Hunting

Livingstone hoped to expand British trade in Africa to help end the slave trade. Stanley's original purpose in heading to Africa was to sell newspapers.

### Did you know?

The Nile River has two branches. The Blue Nile begins in Ethiopia. Nineteenth-century British explorers were searching for the source of the White Nile, which is longer but not as wide.

## AN IMPERIAL PRIZE

★ **Following the Nile**

★ **Britain seeks trade route**

During the late 1800s, European countries competed for power in Africa. Britain hoped to find a trade route from the heart of Africa to the Mediterranean. They believed the Nile (right) might provide that route, and British explorers set out to find the river's source. Livingstone's attempts to solve the mystery of the Nile's source made him a hero to **patriotic** Britons.

## STOP THE SLAVE TRADE

**+ Livingstone fights slavery**

After his first trip across Africa ended in 1856, Livingstone became famous, and as a result was able to raise funds for more exploration. He was eager to open up possibilities for trade other than slavery (left), which he campaigned against. The possibility of increased trade attracted money from the British government—and the public— for Livingstone's expedition to the Zambezi in 1858.

# READ ALL ABOUT IT!

- Circulation war in the United States

- Editor wants more readers

In 1869, James Gordon Bennett was the editor of the *New York Herald*. He realized that the story of what had happened to David Livingstone, who was then missing, could help him sell more newspapers in the United States (below). He paid for Stanley's expedition to find Livingstone, and the paper's **circulation** soared.

## My Explorer Journal

★ **Imagine you are Henry Stanley and you are writing about finding Livingstone. Write three headlines for the newspaper to get people to read your story.**

# STANLEY GETS A JOB

★ **Stanley makes headline news**

Stanley became famous after finding Livingstone in Ujiji. He claimed that his first words to the explorer were, "Dr. Livingstone, I presume?" The words became legendary. Stanley's success even caught the attention of the Belgian king, Leopold II. Leopold hired Stanley to establish a **colony** in an area of western Africa called the Congo.

# TRENDING NOW: LIVINGSTONE IN AFRICA

- Book a bestseller

- Livingstone becomes a hero

Livingstone based his first book, *Missionary Travels and Researches in South Africa* (1857, right), on the journals he kept. It was a huge hit. Readers in Britain and across Europe loved to read the tales about African culture, exotic animals, and landscapes.

# This Isn't What It Said in the Brochure!

During his 30 years in Africa, Livingstone endured sickness, animal attacks, and danger. Stanley also faced sickness and difficult moments during his search for Livingstone.

> " He caught me by the shoulder and we both came to the ground together. Growling horribly he shook me as a terrier dog does a rat."
> *Livingstone describes the lion attack.*

## ATTACK OF THE BIG CAT

- A lion strikes
- Livingstone permanently injured

While at Mabotsa with the Bakgatla people in 1844, Livingstone had a terrifying encounter in the bush. A lion attacked him, crushing and biting his arm. The lion also attacked two more men before one of the Bakgatla men shot and killed it. Livingstone's arm was permanently damaged.

## MASSACRE AT NYANGWE

★ Hundreds murdered on market day

Nyangwe was an Arab trading post and market town where Livingstone stayed in 1871. There was a lot of tension between the Arabs and the local Africans. One market day, violence erupted. The Arabs fired at local people who tried to get away by canoe. Hundreds died, most of them women. The next day, the Arabs attacked and set fire to local villages. Horrified and scared, Livingstone returned to Ujiji on Lake Tanganyika, where he had previously stayed.

# STRUCK DOWN BY DISEASE

- Explorers struck down
- Both come close to death

Both Stanley and Livingstone suffered from terrible diseases such as dysentery and malaria. Livingstone also suffered from near starvation, and got terrible sores on his feet and legs. He had to be carried (right), or sometimes was too sick to move. On his last journey in 1869, Livingstone fell ill from pneumonia and was sick for five months. He did not make it far before falling sick again with his final illness.

## Thieves

Early in his African career, thieves stole vital medicine from David Livingstone. Later, robbers stole his supplies more than once, and left him nearly starving. Stanley met with similar problems.

# NOTHING LEFT

+ Stanley reaches Ujiji...

+ ... finds Livingstone with nothing left

The most famous moment in Livingstone's career was also one of the worst. On November 10, 1871, he was at Ujiji. He was frail and sick. His supplies had been stolen and most of his money was gone. Then Stanley arrived with supplies, and flying the American flag (above). Relieved, Livingstone said to Stanley, "I feel thankful that I am here to welcome you."

# End of the Road

Although Livingstone and Stanley spent little time together, their historic meeting linked their names forever. They enjoyed different fortunes afterward.

## Funeral

The British government gave David Livingstone an official state funeral in honor of his exploration in Africa. He became the first explorer to be buried in Westminster Abbey, London.

## DEATH IN AFRICA

- ☛ Explorer dies at Chief Chitambo's village
- ☛ Found kneeling in prayer

Stanley and Livingstone spent a month exploring around northern Lake Tanganyika before Stanley left in March 1872. Livingstone traveled south to search for the Nile's source. Sick with dysentery and malaria, Livingstone died during the night on May 1, 1873 in a village near Lake Bangweulu, in modern Zambia. In the morning, Chuma and Susi found his body kneeling next to the bed (right).

## GOING HOME

- ★ Livingstone's body returns to England
- ★ Chuma and Susi take care of Livingstone

After Livingstone died, an African doctor removed his heart and **mummified** his body to preserve it. Chuma and Susi buried the heart at the base of a tree. They then carried Livingstone's body to the coast, from where it was sent to Zanzibar. A relief expedition collected Livingstone's journals and letters at Ujiji. The explorer's body finally reached England in April 1874.

# FAME AND GLORY

**+ Stanley makes his mark**

After Stanley found Livingstone, he hoped the British would welcome him. Instead, some doubted his version of events, while others resented US involvement in a British story. Meanwhile, the Americans hailed him as a hero. Stanley's book, *How I Found Livingstone*, was a bestseller. He returned to Africa and crossed the continent between 1874 and 1877. He settled in Britain and became a member of Parliament. In 1899, Stanley received a knighthood for his services to the British Empire.

# A NEW AFRICA

**☞ Exploration changes history**

**☞ Europeans take control of Africa**

The expeditions of Livingstone and Stanley helped spark the "Scramble for Africa." In the late 1800s, European nations competed to set up colonies in Africa (right). By 1913, the whole continent was ruled by Europe, from British South Africa to French West Africa and the Belgian Congo. In spite of good intentions, such as ending the slave trade, Livingstone and Stanley helped create an Africa ruled by and **exploited** by European powers.

# CONTROVERSIAL CAREER

**★ Cruelty in the Congo**

**★ Stanley opens the door for Belgians**

Stanley's exploration of the Congo in western Africa was supported by Leopold II, the king of Belgium (right). Leopold claimed the Congo and its resources, particularly rubber and ivory. The Belgians treated the Congolese with great brutality. This era damaged Stanley's reputation, and tales spread about Stanley's own mistreatment of Africans. People still argue about the extent of Stanley's cruelty to his porters and others.

# GLOSSARY

**ally** A person who cooperates with another

**altitude** The height of a location above ground or sea level

**baptized** Admitted into the Christian church

**botanist** A scientist who studies plants

**caravan** A group of people traveling together

**chronometer** A highly accurate clock

**circulation** The number of copies of a newspaper that are bought

**colonization** The process by which countries take control of other territories

**colony** A region governed by another country

**compass** A device with a magnetized needle that indicates the direction of north

**convert** To give up one religion for another, or to persuade someone else to do so

**dysentery** An infection that causes severe diarrhea

**exploited** Made maximum use of, often in an unfair way

**gourds** Fleshy fruit with hard skin

**interior** The part of a continent inland from the coast

**irrigation** Artificially watering land to grow crops

**ivory** A hard, creamy-white substance obtained from elephant tusks

**malaria** An often deadly mosquito-borne fever

**medicine men** Doctors who use traditional methods of healing

**missionary** A person who promotes a religion in a foreign country

**missions** Buildings where missionaries live

**mummified** Dried out for preservation

**ordained** Made a minister of a church

**patriotic** Having a great love of one's country

**porter** Someone employed to carry a load

**rapids** A fast-flowing, rocky stretch of a river

**scalpel** A sharp knife used by a surgeon

**scoop** A story a newspaper reports before anyone else

**sextant** A device for measuring the height of objects above the horizon

**stethoscope** A device for listening to the heart

**workhouse** A place where poor people were forced to work in return for food and lodging

---

**May:** David Livingstone arrives in southern Africa to work as a missionary.

Livingstone builds a mission at Kolobeng. He meets the Bakwena leader Sechele, who becomes a Christian the following year.

**May 20:** After three years of traveling, Livingstone completes his crossing of Africa from west to east.

**March:** Livingstone sets out to explore the Zambezi River. The six-year mission proves a failure, and is canceled by the British government in 1864.

**1841    1845    1847    1855    1856    1858    1862**

**January:** Livingstone marries Mary Moffat, daughter of the missionary Robert Moffat; the couple will have six children.

**November 16:** Livingstone becomes the first European to see the spectacular falls he names Victoria Falls.

**July 30:** British explorer John Hanning Speke reaches Lake Victoria, which he identifies as the source of the Nile River.

**April 27:** Mary Livingstone dies of malaria near Lake Malawi.

# ON THE WEB

**livingstone.library.ucla.edu/
1871diary/index.htm**
UCLA's digital exhibition about Livingstone's
1871 diary.

**www.eyewitnesstohistory.com/
livingstone.htm**
Livingstone's own account of finding the
Victoria Falls.

**www.newworldencyclopedia.org/
entry/David_Livingstone**
New World Encyclopedia entry on Livingstone,
with a timeline.

**www.livingstoneonline.org/**
A comprehensive site about Livingstone's life
the and research into his achievements.

**www.westminster-abbey.org/our-
history/people/david-livingstone**
The story of Livingstone's burial and grave from
Westminster Abbey in London.

**www.bbc.co.uk/history/historic_
figures/stanley_sir_henry morton.
shtml**
A BBC History biography of Henry Stanley.

**www.eyewitnesstohistory.com/
stanley.htm**
Stanley's own account of his meeting with
Livingstone at Ujiji.

# BOOKS

Freedman, Frances. *David Livingstone* (World
Explorers). World Almanac Library, 2002.

Golding, Vautier. *The Story of David Livingstone*
(The Children's Heroes). Yesterday's Classics, 2007.

Otfinoski, Steven. *David Livingstone: Deep in the
Heart of Africa* (Great Explorations). Cavendish
Square Publishing, 2006.

Worth, Richard. *Stanley and Livingstone and the
Exploration of Africa in World History*. Enslow
Publishers, 2000.

**March 19:** Livingstone leaves Zanzibar to find the source of the Nile—little more is heard from him.

**February 5:** Stanley sets out from Zanzibar with a huge expedition.

**November 11:** Stanley finds Livingstone, sick and poor, at Ujiji on Lake Tanganyika.

**May 1:** Susi and Chuma find Livingstone dead in a position of prayer in a village named Chitambo.

**May 10:** Sir Henry Stanley, who has been knighted in 1899, dies in London.

**1866** **1869** **1871** **1872** **1873** **1877** **1904**

**October 11:** A letter from Africa reports the presence of a white man at Ujiji on Lake Tanganyika.

**October 27:** American newspaper editor James Gordon Bennett sends Henry Stanley to Africa to find Livingstone.

**March 14:** After exploring Lake Tanganyika with Livingstone, Stanley leaves to return to Zanzibar.

**August 9:** Stanley arrives at the west coast of Africa after a four-year journey from the east coast.

# INDEX